# THE ART
# OF HOME

# SARA
# STORY

# THE ART OF HOME

# SARA STORY

WRITTEN WITH JUDITH NASATIR

*RIZZOLI*
NEW YORK

New York Paris London Milan

For **KEN, DUKE, EDWARD,** and **DAGNY.**
Wherever you are is **HOME** for me.

# CONTENTS

# MY STORY

I am a homebody, but I love to travel. In some ways, I live for travel. But always, no matter how incredible the trip is, I cannot wait to come home. Home is my cocoon, the place where I recharge. When I entertain, I'd rather stay home than go out. I gather people at my house. For dinner parties. For cocktail parties. For games. For coffee. For a visit. I always have my family with me, and I bring in my friends. This is the way I like to live. And it's why I believe home is so important.

Personal. Meaningful. Engaging. Cozy. Comfortable. Fun. Happy. Whimsical. Curated. Edited. These are the kinds of interiors that I love, and that I work to create for my family and my clients. My preference is to mix vintage, contemporary, and commissioned pieces. It matters to me that each element of the room is unique, and that each piece serves both a practical and artistic purpose. Art, accessories, and collections of favorite items play an important role in my rooms because they come with their own histories and stories, and become part of our stories, too.

My goal is to create spaces that gently present themselves, that only gradually reveal their logic. Success is when someone says sixth months after they've moved in: "Now I understand why the material and shape of this coffee table make sense, how they relate to the lamp and work with the seating and the art, how everything is interwoven."

I was born in Japan. My family moved to Singapore a few years later. When I was six, we moved to Texas, my parents' home state, settling in the Houston suburbs. We were different than most families I grew up with. Our house was filled with the things that my parents had collected in Singapore, Japan, and Thailand, where they had lived before I was

born. Wood block prints, vintage textiles, ikats, lacquer pieces, old baskets—my parents loved it all. Our furniture was in the same vein.

My fascination with art started early. Art was part of my mother's world and repertoire because she worked for Houston's contemporary art museum. I remember her taking me to museums and putting me in art classes. She also painted beautiful watercolors. By exposing me to so much, so early, she was an enormous influence on my eye and my taste. Her aesthetic sensibility was very pared down, very tactile, natural, and raw. I love the serene and the organic, too. But contrast speaks to me, so I will mix in lacquer, shine, and metals to create a telling juxtaposition. Even from an early age, I took an interest in what my room was like, redoing, mixing everything around, even painting my floor.

I always wanted to see the world. In college, I studied psychology because it fascinated me. I never thought about interior design as a profession until I was living in San Francisco after graduation. I was selling software to architects and designers and realized that sales and marketing were not for me. I went back to school and got a degree in interior architecture at the Academy of Art University in San Francisco. During an internship in an architect's office—she was amazing, and I still remember how cool the models were—I knew I had found my future. Soon after, I met my husband and moved to New York.

Before I opened my own firm, I worked in Victoria Hagan's office for three years. Talk about smart and talented. She taught me that for a design business to be successful, it had to be very efficient and professional. She insisted that everything that went out of the office had to be perfect: wrapped in tissue paper, cover letter enclosed, in a white bag with a beautifully addressed label. She also had her own design rules, and her style influenced me, of course. When I went out on my own, it was time to define my voice as a designer.

Travel has been my most important teacher and my greatest inspiration. Growing up, my family traveled throughout Asia, but not to Europe. I remember being in Paris for the first time and starting to discover, well, all of design again from an entirely new perspective: interiors, materials, colors, patterns, architecture, scale, history, you name it. Spending time in Provence was another kind of revelation: the stone houses with concrete floors, updated with steel-and-glass windows and wooden slats to filter the sun; the juxtapositions and mixing of periods inside, where classical and vintage pieces felt right at home with contemporary art. I became obsessed with Copenhagen while reading about the restaurant Noma and the Louisiana Museum of Modern Art. When I visited for the first time, I was completely captivated. Everything was so austere, but so warm, and I was amazed by the materials, the design history, and the craftsmanship. I have an ongoing love affair with Turkey, the cities and landscapes of South America, and Africa. Milan is my latest passion, and such an eye-opener every time I go.

I believe in setting goals. I am fascinated by people who push themselves to their limits, who dig deep to find the discipline necessary to accomplish whatever challenge they set for themselves, whether it's building the house of their dreams, climbing Mount Kilimanjaro, or unlocking a mystery of science. You have to be inspired. I have to be inspired. I crave the feeling of going deeper and deeper into what excites my eyes and my senses, of being so wrapped up in a place, a painting, a project that everything else disappears until I bring those experiences home, and into the art of home.

**THIS HOUSE IS A MÉLANGE,** but it's **COMFORTABLE** and **COZY,** with lots of **COLOR** and **PATTERN** on the walls, and filled with our **FAMILY LIFE.** Our children **LOVE** it. We've been accumulating this place—the spaces, the furnishings, the collections, the art—over eighteen years. **EVERYTHING IN IT HAS MEMORIES.** No matter where we are in the world, we always want to come **HOME.**

Before I married my husband, I had never lived in New York City. His apartment, right in the heart of Midtown, was too loud for me. The only other part of Manhattan he would consider was Gramercy Park. We found our first apartment in this townhouse when I was seven months pregnant. It had just undergone a beautiful renovation, and it was perfect: a one-bedroom with a closet big enough to convert for the baby. Gradually, as we expanded our family, we began to cobble together other units in the building, hoping in time to reunite the entire house. Each time we added another, I would paint, put up light fixtures, pull together some furniture. **I FELT FREE BECAUSE I THOUGHT, "I'LL JUST DO EACH NEW SPACE FAST. AND AT SOME POINT, I'LL RENOVATE THE WHOLE HOUSE."**

I love **VINTAGE PIECES.** And **WHAT I CAN'T FIND, I DESIGN.** I'm **OBSESSED WITH MATERIALS.** And **THE POP OF COLOR.** I'm really attracted to **LARGE-SCALE ART.** And I always have to have **SOMETHING REALLY WHIMSICAL.** I have so many **LITTLE COLLECTIONS.** My parents traveled all over the world, so they would bring me things like antique Mongolian bowls. My father would always find me gorgeous objects to do with smoking and matches. I am crazy about ceramics, so I scout new artists and pick up vessels whenever I'm in Asia and Europe.

CREATION STORY

I think of the **SECOND FLOOR** almost like **AN ARTIST'S SALON,** and we often use it in that classic way, as our **RECEPTION ROOMS** for **ENTERTAINING.** It's the original parlor floor, with the most beautiful architecture: perfect scale and ceiling height, plus doors, windows, and original moldings from the 1840s. The crystal chandeliers (which were here, and which I love though I wouldn't have chosen them) and the gilt mirrors make the living area feel very European. Every time I look at Per Barclay's photograph of a Swiss bank vault that hangs above the sofa, I see so much of what also fascinates me about New York: the beauty in the utilitarian, the city as a financial center, and the power of the grid. I always think that behind every one of those drawers lies a story of family and history, of secrets and valuables.

**WHENEVER I DESIGN SOMETHING FOR A ROOM, I HOPE TO GIVE THAT ROOM A POINT OF VIEW.** We eat together as a family as much as possible, and we'd rather host a dinner party than go out, so tables are key. The instant I saw the colorful terrazzo in Europe, I knew I had to create a table for our dining room with it as the tabletop. For the base, I took inspiration from the legs of Jean Prouvé's furniture. The chairs by Gio Ponti are my favorite chairs ever, small in scale but so comfortable, and visually open so you can see all the intricacies involved in the structure of the table. Our kitchen table, the site of family dinners night after night for eighteen years, is a Chinese antique made from a single piece of wood. Talk about sturdy. And about longevity.

I still want to renovate, but we have so many memories in these rooms. **IT'S HOME.**

PAGE 9: The combination of feminine and masculine elements makes our third-floor sitting room a favorite retreat. **PAGE 13:** Contrast keeps interiors interesting. Artwork by Elizabeth Peyton stands out against the dark walls of the smoking room off our living room. **PREVIOUS PAGES:** Built as a single-family residence in 1844, our house was later broken up into apartments that we've gradually put back together. The parlor floor, now our formal living room, retains much of its original detail. **OPPOSITE:** African walking sticks add bold geometries to the nature-inspired architectural ornament.

**PREVIOUS PAGES, LEFT:** The marble top of the living room's 1970s French coffee table speaks the same graphic language as the Moroccan rug. The lacquer vessel is from Laos. **PREVIOUS PAGES, RIGHT:** With Martin Eisler's iconic midcentury Brazilian lounge chair, lamp by Paavo Tynell, and layered rugs, this living room corner offers a quiet spot for reading. The painting is by Sean Scully. **RIGHT:** The vintage Swedish sectional creates such a comfortable gathering place for groups both large and small. Pillows dressed in Fortuny fabrics add both pattern and sheen. Isamu Noguchi's Akari lamp, which casts such a soft, warm glow when lit, is a piece of functional sculpture. Per Barclay's photograph of a Swiss bank vault interior picks up on the reflection and shine. I designed a lacquer pedestal in the adjacent smoking room to give the ceramic by Timothée Humbert the prominence it deserves. The crystal chandeliers and tall mirrors that give these rooms their European flavor were existing.

**ABOVE:** There's something completely magical about Morocco. A trip there inspired the tile installation and red lacquer in this bath. The wood block prints are from Venice. **OPPOSITE:** A de Gournay wallcovering helps give my home office a serene, thoughtful atmosphere with an artistic flair. The French antique desk is a find from Argentina. Marcel Breuer's Bauhaus classic cantilevered chair is truly comfortable.

**OPPOSITE:** Florals are not usually my go-to, but the Josef Frank wallpaper that wraps our game room works beautifully with the crown molding because of the way the flower forms echo each other. The zig-zag pattern in the floor was existing.
**ABOVE:** The work by Nancy Lorenz above the fireplace layers in notes of both the rustic and the refined, and a little shine, too.

PREVIOUS PAGES: Jermaine Gallacher candlesticks carry the terrazzo colors up into space (LEFT) and a painting by Kati Heck inserts a form of social commentary (RIGHT). ABOVE: The blue of the velvet threads through our entertaining spaces. I designed the table's forms with my favorite Gio Ponti chair in mind. OPPOSITE: I love large-scale art. I also love how smaller works like this Cecily Brown painting can draw focus. The floor lamp is a vintage find.

# PLOT POINTS

The formulaic is not for me. And I never want to repeat myself. I strive to find interesting things. Unusual things. Unique things. Things that spark that connection between the eye, the intellect, and the emotion. That stop me in my tracks, grab my imagination, and won't let go. When I do, I leap. Then I dig in deep to discover the story, to find out every detail I can about the person who made the item and the thought process, materials, and techniques that went into its creation.

Creativity and craftsmanship go hand in hand when the goal is to make something that is singular. I go to galleries everywhere I travel, investigate their roster of artists and artisans, then work to get a grasp on their ideas. I love to discover talents on the rise who aren't yet represented by the big galleries and whose work isn't everywhere. I am always looking for that spark of possibility, for an interesting idea and its potential application for a project.

There is nothing better—or more exciting—than collaborating with talented artisans and makers.

I always have a vision of what I want. They inevitably amplify it. Together, we work to bring it into being. In the process of its making, it inevitably becomes more than we had imagined.

This is true whether I am working with an amazing Japanese textile artist on weaving curtain fabrics, a fabulous South African wood carver on a coffee table shaped from a solid block of tree trunk, an incredible Belgian craftsperson on developing leather panels interlaced with other fibers and materials to set into millwork, or a remarkable glass artist to create églomisé tiles for a backsplash. Our conversations drill down into the very essence of art and design: the shape of a leaf in a pattern, the quality of texture and hand, what's right for an ombré border—all the nuances of materials and scale and detail, of visual and practical sense. These kinds of challenges, and the learning process that they bring with them, are what make interior design so fun, interesting, and creative.

30

PAGE 31: In the bar of the smoking room, Laotian lacquer-ware speaks to the antique Asian games table. **PREVIOUS PAGES:** In our family room, the super comfortable Mario Bellini modular sofa is roomy enough for all five of us to hang out together. I found the etched brass table in Europe and the vintage lounge chairs in the Netherlands. Video art by Ragnar Kjartansson and the antique Chinese monk figures feel very neighborly. The chandelier by Wade Guytan and Kelley Walker brings a touch of elegant whimsy. Above the mantel, a ceramic by Shio Kusaka, left, and two works by Yoshimoto Nara, right, sandwich a work by Matthew Branson. **RIGHT:** I love how the lines of Daniel Richter's monumental painting and the coffee table's etchings echo each other.

**ABOVE, LEFT TO RIGHT:** The family room's mélange includes an Eric Crowes ceramic beneath a piece by Tal R; antique Asian ceramics; my vintage match strikers; and a bronze side table by Eric Crowes atop a cowhide rug.
**FOLLOWING PAGES, LEFT:** We eat as many family meals as possible around our antique Asian elmwood kitchen table.
**FOLLOWING PAGES, RIGHT:** A *Mona Lisa* by Gelitin reposes above one of our Chinese lacquer hat chairs.

PREVIOUS PAGES, LEFT: The de Gournay china helps enliven this essentially neutral room. PREVIOUS PAGES, RIGHT: The stenciled floor adds a grounding of geometry. Ruan Hoffmann's ceramics hang on the wall. ABOVE AND OPPOSITE: Paneled walls that hide a working kitchen create another, more intimate dining room. A Bubble Lamp designed by George Nelson fits the mid-century mood. Anonymous portraits stand in for, and send up, those in traditional paneled dining rooms.

PAGES 44–45: Our bedroom is nested in the trees. The Hervé van der Straeten lantern suggests twigs; the Jean Royère floor lamp, branches. Friedrich Kunath's work above the mantel feels well wedded with Alison Blickle's above a custom Roman Thomas sideboard.
PREVIOUS PAGES: In our sitting room, the curved and the cornered happily cohabit. Miriam Ellner's églomisé panel layers in reflection.
ABOVE: BZippy's vessel introduces interesting texture. OPPOSITE: José Lerma's painting happily blasts in color and form.

I want every house I design to be **BEAUTIFUL AT FIRST GLANCE,** but also to have **HIDDEN DEPTHS** of design, so that **THE MORE YOU LOOK AND EXPERIENCE THE SPACES, THE MORE YOU UNCOVER.** These longtime clients, amazing entrepreneurs, have very specific taste and love the creative process. Like me, they believe that a perfect piece is something that's practical but also an amazing element in the room that's created by an artist. This shared idea became a kind of throughline for this project, our fourth together, a gut renovation of a one-story that was then built up, not out, because of building restrictions in their Los Angeles neighborhood.

The original floor plan was wide open, and the dimensions of the spaces were a bit awkward. We had been working on various iterations of a screen inspired by Eileen Gray's iconic 1922 design **TO DIFFERENTIATE THE LIVING AND DINING AREAS** when the owners fell in love with one by Mark Hagen at the Hammer Museum. The **MOLDED CONCRETE SCREEN THAT WE COMMISSIONED** from Hagen does the job brilliantly—so much so that it's like **A METAPHOR FOR THE ENTIRE DESIGN,** not only because it's a functional element made by an artist specifically for its location, but also because it frames glimpses of the space that then resolve into the larger picture.

These two just love **TEXTURE,** so the living area is based on a **NUBBY WOOL** and **SILK** rug, with soft rolls of **COTTON VELVET** on the sofa. Because this space is so long—long enough for three seating groups—I wanted to add **CEILING BEAMS** to create definition and a sense of intimacy. We lined the powder room in **JAPANESE PAPER PAINTED BY HAND** and chose a **MARBLE WITH A LOT OF MOVEMENT** for the vanity. In the main bedrooms, **LUMINOUS PARCHMENT** covers the bed wall.

A STORY

PREVIOUS PAGE: The concrete screen commissioned from Mark Hagen is key to defining the interior's spatial flow and overall aesthetic. THESE PAGES: Beneath a painting by March Avery, the entry vestibule's custom metal console adds contrasting texture in an edgy mix. The sculpture is by Ugo Rondinone.

She spends a lot of time in the kitchen, which made the **LIGHTING** very important. The fixtures over the island are much like those that Adolf Loos used in the Villa Müller in Prague, a house that I find endlessly inspiring. Besides, **A SPHERE IS A PERFECT THING,** and here it blends decoration and function. The ceiling in the primary bedroom is so incredibly high, we needed **A FIXTURE TO ACTIVATE THE AIR SPACE.** The Paavo Tynell design we chose casts an atmospheric light that becomes, well, the ethereal elephant in the room.

These two are as **PASSIONATE ABOUT ART** as I am. They're also **ON THE CUTTING EDGE.** With paintings and sculptures by Sterling Ruby, Ugo Rondinone, Laura Owens, Friedrich Kunath, Jonas Wood, and March Avery, their collection is one of the project's strongest elements. To add detail at a **SMALLER SCALE,** we found many wonderful **CERAMICS,** including pieces by Roger Herman, Shio Kusaka, and Peter Lane.

This couple is just as **ADVENTUROUS** in their **FURNITURE CHOICES.** Along with vintage finds and various pieces we had made, we included furniture by **AVANT-GARDE DESIGNERS:** Ingrid Donat, the Haas Brothers, and Rick Owens, among others. The sexiest of all may be one of the first pieces they bought— a console by Patrick Naggar with optical lenses that can be lit from the inside.

The finished rooms feel much like these homeowners and their Southern California surroundings: **FULL OF LIGHT,** with **A SOFT, NEUTRAL PALETTE,** and lots of **BOLD, FRESH ART.**

A Jonathan Browning light fixture hints at lighting motifs to come. Friedrich Kunath's painting brings gorgeous color, and more, into the space.

**PREVIOUS PAGES:** This living room is large enough for three seating areas. At one end, works by Sam Falls, left, Brenna Youngblood, center, and Jordon Wolfson, right, surround custom sofas centered on a Rick Owens coffee table. **ABOVE:** The middle seating area spins off the custom travertine fireplace surround; pieces by Ed Ruscha rest on the mantel. An Achille Salvagni fixture hovers above. **OPPOSITE:** Antoinette Faragallah's ceramic vase adds texture to the coffee table.

CRISIS OF DESIRE
David Hockney Portraits
JAMES TURRELL
KRYLON
SPRAY PAINT
WILLIAM EGGLESTON BEFORE COLOR STEIDL
Basquiat
Mark Bradford
ECHO
INDIA
GOLF
HOTEL
TANGO
HAAS BROTHE
Internationa
Andy Coolquitt
Simon Baker GEORG

**PREVIOUS PAGES:** Added ceiling beams break up the long living room space. In the third seating area, a custom sectional centers on a library wall of custom millwork with a concealed TV. French 1940s chairs by René Gabriel round out the group. **ABOVE:** Carefully set shelves frame artworks and books. **OPPOSITE:** Between vintage sconces, a Sterling Ruby painting floats above a vintage console.

ABOVE, LEFT TO RIGHT: This client loves ceramics as much as I do, so we put together a collection for this house that includes works by Shio Kusaka, Roger Herman, and Cody Hoyt. A coffee table by Ingrid Donat echoes the texture of the screen. PAGE 66: The textures, forms, and materials in this corner tell the design story in a nutshell.

# CHARACTER DEVELOPMENT

I prefer a curated, edited, meaningful interior. For me, this means that each piece must matter. Otherwise, I'd rather not include it.

Perfect pieces to me are functional. At the same time, I consider them art, which means that I see art as not only painting and sculpture, but also ceramics, objects, furnishings, and light fixtures. I tend to gravitate toward a strong point of view. If a work grabs me, pulls me in emotionally and intellectually—and keeps me thinking about it—I need to know who made it and what the rest of that artist's or craftsman's body of work involves. I dig into my research because I want to find out and understand the maker's perspective, trajectory, process, and the meaning behind them. Then I hope to get to know the person behind the piece, to see him or her at home in the studio, if a studio tour is an option.

My love of ceramics comes from my mother, who started collecting pieces as a young bride in Asia. She took me to ceramic shows. She taught me to see a different kind of beauty, an "ugly" beauty, deep beneath the surface. She used to give me ceramics, particularly gnarled Japanese ceramics, as gifts. I always liked them. But I love them so much more now that I understand that their makers were not attempting "perfection" but exploiting its opposite. These pieces celebrate the aesthetic power of imperfection and the fact that the kiln is where this art of the irregular, of challenging forms and glazes, occurs. I find an arresting grace in that idea.

I love that art can tell stories, that it can keep us looking and thinking. I am always amazed at the way art makes connections: to places and experiences we hope to discover or want to remember, to ideas or feelings we may experience for the first time or cherish for a lifetime, even just to favorite colors, materials, textures, patterns, and finishes. I do believe everything in a home should be useful and serve a purpose. But rooms and homes without interesting objects feel lifeless to me. I prefer to have just one piece of art—or furniture or object—that I really love, or nothing at all.

PREVIOUS PAGES: The hand meets the machined in this dining room. Behind the Belgian oak table, a Patrick Naggar console hosts ceramics by the Haas Brothers. Paintings by Laura Owens, left, and Jonas Wood bring joy. **ABOVE:** An ombré mirror rises above the powder room's custom vanity. **OPPOSITE:** Hermès fabric covers an heirloom English chair in the husband's study. The rug is by Joseph La Piana; the painting, by Jake Longstreth.

OPPOSITE: The wife, a tremendous cook, uses her kitchen constantly so she insisted that it function just as beautifully as it looks. The marble island combines a kitchen table with the cooktop, keeping the workspace close but comfortably separate from the seating area. The overhead lights are from Masters of Modernism. FOLLOWING PAGES: In the adjacent dining area, the chairs around the custom table help bring playful colors into the neutral space. The ceiling fixture mirrors the geometry of the table's legs. A painting by Nicolas Party hangs at the base of the stair, which, with its glass wall, is actually a three-story lightwell. The painting on the right is by Aaron Garber-Maikovska.

With its view of the olive trees that surround the pool, this primary bedroom makes the most of the seamless indoor/outdoor connection that defines the California lifestyle. We kept the focus on the view with a serene, neutral palette and rich, luminous textures. The bed wall is lined with parchment panels that glow at all times of the day and night. So delicate, the ceiling fixture by Paavo Tynell casts the most enchanting shadows when it's lit.

ORIGIN STORY

When my sisters and I were young, our **FAMILY GETAWAY** was a one-room cabin my father had built in **TEXAS HILL COUNTRY.** I never thought I would put down roots there, but my husband fell in love with it the first time I brought him home to meet my parents before we were married. Once we pieced together a spread next to my father's, we commissioned Lake | Flato, the firm that created his traditional ranch, to design a **MODERN RANCH** for us. They often take inspiration from the work of Frank Lloyd Wright and Tadao Ando. I also gave them images of favorite projects by Ludwig Mies van der Rohe, Richard Neutra, and other twentieth-century greats. They developed a plan with a **FORMAL GEOMETRY,** situated the house beautifully between existing stands of oak trees, and incorporated **LOCAL MATERIALS,** like Lueders limestone, in the construction. There are **JAPANESE INFLUENCES,** including the rain chains, which are commonly used in Japan instead of downspouts. The steel-and-glass windows are favorite details of the renovated farmhouses where we've stayed in Provence. I like my interiors a little **MORE AUSTERE,** so I stuck mostly to the basics of **BLACK, WHITE, AND GRAY.** But I never want any area to feel too fancy to **ENJOY** or **RELAX** in.

**LIGHTING IS MY SWEET SPOT,** and often **HOW I BEGIN** my interiors. This house is a composition of lighting with many **DIFFERENT IDEAS OF HOW TO FILTER** and **DIRECT** and **SHAPE** and **MODULATE IT.** Lighting for me is **ALSO A KIND OF JEWELRY.** It took me time to figure out what to do at the entry, which is shaped by massive limestone blocks. I felt the fixture should be like a sculpture. The design by Vincenzo De Cotiis with its hanging rods, has that feel. In the dining room, the Studio Drift dandelion chandelier is in the shape of Texas, which you only see in the evening when it's lit and reflects in the window. When I saw the artists, I asked them if this resemblance was intentional, but they said they

had no idea. The pendants over the kitchen island sheath the bulbs in perforated metal cylinders that attach to crystal spheres. One of my favorites, a brass fixture, by Paavo Tynell, adds whimsy above **THE BREAKFAST TABLE, WHICH RECREATES A FAVORITE MEMORY.** When my sisters and I were growing up, we ate all our meals with our mother at a small marble-topped table, like a tea shop table, sitting on Thonet chairs like the vintage ones here.

I wanted to include **AN INTERESTING MATERIAL ON EVERY ELEVATION,** and a **MORE NUANCED, CONTEMPORARY** take on the limestone—something that wasn't expected or typical, from horsehair-wrapped panels in the study to églomisé in the kitchen. An artisan in New York City worked for more than a year to create the eggshell wall panels in the living room. Up close, they have the same kind of forms as the stone. Some walls in the primary bedroom are honed limestone. Some are perforated suede. It's just so **COZY,** and a nice **CONTRAST,** especially against the oak headboard with its metal inlay, leather bedside tables, brushed velvet on the bench, and the raw silk curtains, made by an incredible weaver I found in Laos.

I like **REALLY BIG ART.** And **I HAVE A LOT HERE,** which is such **A LUXURY.** For me, art brings in whimsy and color. **THE NEUTRAL SPACES FEEL SO SERENE, AND THE COLOR MAKES YOU HAPPY.**

PAGE 78: Jojo and Janou have the run of the property. PREVIOUS PAGES: The living room's quiet palette lets the artwork and views speak. A René Gabriel lounge chair and Vincenzo De Cotiis coffee table layer in forms and materials. A Neo Rauch painting dominates one wall. OPPOSITE: Hand-crafted eggshell panels shine softly around the blackened steel fireplace. The custom sectional combines boiled wool, velvet, cashmere, leather, and silk embroidery.

PREVIOUS PAGES: The wall of honed Lueders limestone creates an interesting contrast with the eggshell and steel opposite and provides a fantastic backdrop for the large photograph by Thomas Ruff. It also creates an organic frame for the sculpture by Ugo Rondinone that we used to create a focal point in the landscape. THESE PAGES: Cut from the earth and reshaped by hand, raw blocks of Lueders limestone that clad the exterior of the house feel just as timeless, full of spirit, and at home as Rondinone's sculpture.

PREVIOUS PAGES: The Jacques Adnet chairs that surround our custom onyx, oak, and lacquer dining table include two vintage originals found in Paris with others I had made to complete the set. A painting by Nicolas Party hangs above a Raymond Loewy sideboard.
ABOVE, LEFT TO RIGHT: Peaches from our orchard make a delectable centerpiece. The leather rug features metal stitching. The petite Japanese ceramic vessels comment on the lamp's brass details. Our Studio Drift chandelier mimics the shape of the state of Texas.

PREVIOUS PAGES: To me, the various blacks of the soapstone, steel, and leather combine with the dark wood, open shelves, and shoji screen–like cabinet fronts to give the kitchen a Japanese feel. ABOVE: I discovered Timothée Humbert's ceramics in Provence. Could our peaches look any more ravishing than they do in his dish? OPPOSITE: My mother adored Royal Copenhagen; I've continued to add to her collection.

PREVIOUS PAGES, LEFT: Our breakfast room mimics the setting of my childhood meals with vintage Thonet chairs and a made-for-this-spot table inspired by the café table my sisters and I grew up with. A work by Otis Jones and a Paavo Tynell ceiling fixture add punctuation. PREVIOUS PAGES, RIGHT: Tyler Hays's ceramics add notes of polish to the rustic elegance of a Japanese felted vase. THESE PAGES: Sliding screens frame views from our covered dining and lounging patio out to a reflecting pool and peach orchard beyond. The wood lounge chairs, sofa, and dining table are my designs. A ceramic wall installation by Peter Lane speaks to the raw limestone opposite. FOLLOWING PAGES: A manicured lawn stretches off the patio in both directions. A rain chain inserts a delicate but functional filigree into the view.

PREVIOUS PAGES: Our bedroom is an oasis of calm, with luxurious quiet neutrals balanced by patterns and art. A Japanese textile artist custom wove the silk curtains. A work by Kati Heck hangs on honed limestone.

OPPOSITE: Suede panels subtly transform one wall. Eileen Gray's classic Transat chair is a favorite. ABOVE: My leather-wrapped end tables bring in more texture. The artwork on these pages is by Tomasz Kowalski.

**ABOVE, LEFT TO RIGHT:** Our bath is a complex of connected indoor and outdoor spaces. All the wood elements
are finished with a traditional Japanese process called Shou Sugi Ban, a weatherproofing method
that first chars the wood then coats it with natural oil. The interior shower is lined in plaster. The marble slabs
add understated pattern. My parents gave me the antique Chinese shop sign that hangs above the bath.

**OPPOSITE AND ABOVE:** Woven horsehair panels infuse the study with saturated yet nuanced color; the artwork by Barnaby Furnas glows against it. My husband and I have our desks here. The chairs are by Gio Ponti. The silk rug is from Fort Street Studio. **FOLLOWING PAGES:** De Gournay wallpaper and Josef Frank linen bring the garden into our daughter's room. The designs of Tommi Parzinger inspired me to top her custom lacquer bed with brass finials.

**RIGHT:** The playroom spans the indoor/outdoor divide with a custom games table indoors and a lineup of Ping-Pong and foosball tables just on the other side of the glass sliding doors. Vintage Eames chairs and a leather-covered sofa from B&B Italia create comfort and at the same time add hotspots of bright color. Posters from my collection of Marfa memorabilia speak to the Texas setting. Yoshimoto Nara's skateboards are witty and fun. The pendant fixture is by Sylvain Willenz.

**FOLLOWING PAGES:** The pool house, like the main house, lies lightly on the land. Stefan Rinck's sculpture, totemic and timeless, acts like a punctuation point for this part of the property.

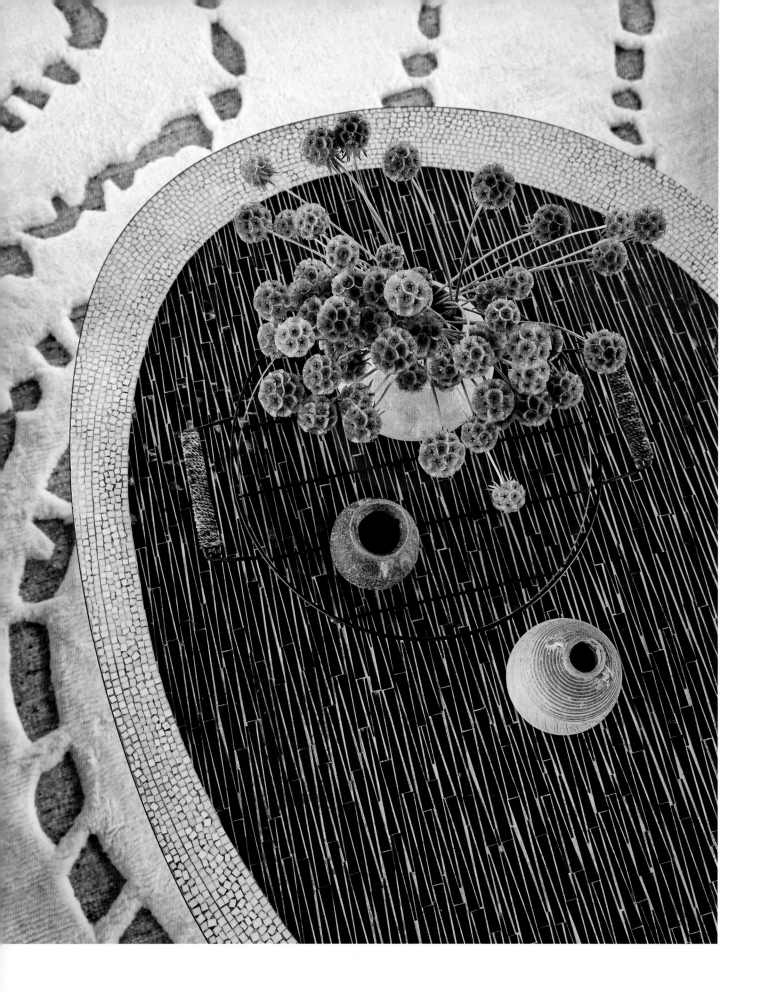

**PREVIOUS PAGES:** The graphic palette becomes lighter inside the pool house. Plush textures and deep upholstered seating create cozy comfort. The antique Thai elephants came from my parents. A work by Otis Jones over the fireplace reinforces the circular shapes that are key to this interior. **ABOVE AND OPPOSITE:** The rug from Woven echoes the coffee table's mosaic motifs. The ceramics I found in Asia.

ABOVE, LEFT TO RIGHT: The architects carefully choreographed the approach with rough limestone walls and honed limestone pavers. Jojo and Janou greet guests at the front door. Vincenzo De Cotiis's sculptural fixture meets the entry's scale. Stands of oak trees dictated the siting of the house. FOLLOWING PAGES: This stair goes to the foosball "field" outside the playroom. A sculpture by Franz West nods to the local wildlife.

# INTERLOCKING STORY

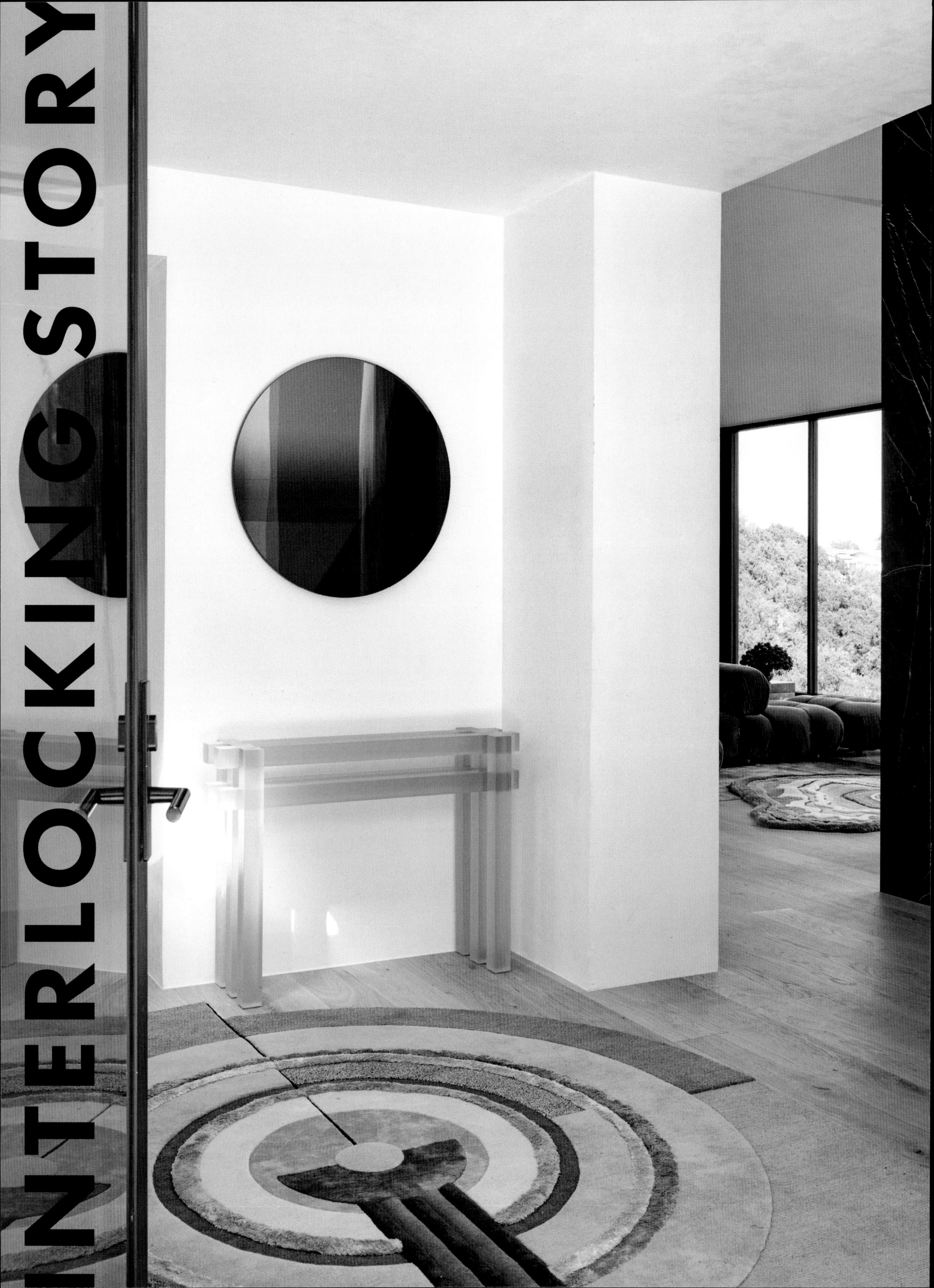

CLIENTS AND PROJECTS THAT PUSH ME TO SEE DIFFERENTLY are also the ones that **TEACH ME THE MOST.** This ranch house perched in the Austin Hills was just this kind of challenge. The client, who entertains often, wanted the interiors to have **A SUPER GROOVY VIBE** (think Lenny Kravitz). He asked for **LOTS OF COLOR—AND AN OPIUM DEN.**

**SOMETIMES** you find just **THE PERFECT PIECE** for an **ENTRY HALL** that **SETS UP** the **ENTIRE DESIGN**—and for this house, the opium den, too. The **MIRROR** by Sabine Marcelis, an artist who plays with reflection, color, form, and material, does that here. She frequently works in resin, **A GREAT STARTING POINT.** She loves aubergines, ambers, ochres, marigold, and terra-cottas—the client's dream palette—which I threaded throughout the house and balanced with black, white, and smoky gray.

To me, **THE DESIGN DNA FOR GROOVY MEANS WAVY LINK PATTERNS AND MODULAR SCULPTURAL FORMS.** In the living room, the sofa by Mario Bellini makes a large statement about shapes at play with the Brazilian chair, vintage lamp, and a Paul Evans side table. In the dining room, we created a sculptural, cast plaster table that echoes the shape of the house. The media room ups the ante with a sheared fur rug with undulating rivulets and curvy sandbars and a wood block coffee table carved by Adam Birch, a South African artist, into solid wiggles—so **ORGANIC, NATURAL, AND WHIMSICAL.**

**WHITE WALLS WERE NOT THE GO-TO FOR THIS CLIENT.** Once we started amping up the vertical surfaces with **COLOR AND PATTERN,** we kept on going—and not just the walls, but **THE CEILINGS, TOO.** A brilliant Japanese

PAINTINGS BY CLARE ROJAS

paper overpainted with an abstract print turns the media room's ceiling into a kind of lacquer box top. Color-wise, it speaks to the screen we commissioned from a pair of artists in California. For the primary bedroom, we brought in a decorative artist whose work I had seen in Milan to paint the walls with a kind of smoke-scape that curls onto the ceiling. The client asked for a color scheme here that matched the gray of a Weimaraner's coat, so we upholstered the low bed in a velvet of that shade. Then we added contrast with black, stacked wood bedside tables by Lucas Castex, a French furniture designer; an enveloping, hand-carved walnut headboard with a Japanese vibe; wavy orange-y sheers made from a fashion textile (used throughout); and ombré curtain panels that transition from aubergine to gray. We gave both guest bedrooms **DYNAMIC** wallcoverings also: one has a **LARGE-SCALE GRAPHIC** and feels almost African; the other is marbled, **PSYCHEDELIC,** and so **HAPPY.**

For the **OPIUM DEN**—the party room that **OPENS TO THE POOL**—the artists who created the mural in the primary bedroom and I came up with a '70s-inspired wall graphic that picks up the swoops and chain-link motifs. We made a niche for the bar by removing millwork, adding an arched opening, and installing a glass panel back painted in the same pattern.

I love that this house has **SUCH A MOOD, SO MUCH ATMOSPHERE.** It's **COMPREHENSIVE**—and **GROOVY**—with **DESIGN CONTINUITY FROM START TO FINISH.**

PAGE 124: Color palette, forms, materials—the main motifs of this 70s-inspired interior jive their way from the entrance into the open-plan living area. A Sabine Marcelis mirror became the fulcrum for all the choices. PREVIOUS PAGES: The living area is a study in curves with an iconic Mario Bellini modular sofa, which allows for open views in all directions; the vintage Italian floor lamp; and the ultra-cool Brazilian chair. OPPOSITE: Mid-century Danish ceramics add organic touches.

# PLACE SETTING

Everybody visits the world differently. Exploring a city makes me come alive. So does setting a new goal or challenge. I crave visual and physical experiences because they give me so much energy—energy, and ideas, that I can then impart to my projects.

Istanbul overwhelmed me on my first visit more than fifteen years ago. The mosaic tiles, relief work, craftsmanship, intricate details, colors, views—all still amaze me when I return. Copenhagen's serene spaces, so warm yet so austere, obsess me. I love Denmark's design history, its heritage of artisanship, great contemporary art, and the way its cities live in their landscapes.

South America and Africa enchant me beyond words. There's a thrill to going off the beaten track, where there are no paved roads, where there's just red dirt as far as the horizon and beyond. The beaches of Uruguay. Patagonia, where you see the wilderness as Charles Darwin did. Chile, with its glaciers and Atacama Desert. Argentina, and especially Buenos Aires, with its European flavor: the palaces, all a little

disheveled, gorgeous moldings still intact, and incredibly detailed hardware that is both hefty and delicate. Africa somehow reminds me of Texas, not in the terrain, but in the spirit. Botswana, South Africa, Mozambique and the surrounding islands. On both continents, I've found amazing artists and craftspeople, and galleries where I continue to shop for clients today. Asia? Whenever I am there, I feel like I am home.

My father used to bring me smoking paraphernalia from his trips to Asia. Later, I started collecting crystal match strikers and ashtrays. It's fun to find the things that represent who you are, what you do, what your hobbies or passions are. It can also be comforting because these objects bring home stories of special moments. They don't have to be man-made. I pick up rocks, chunks of coral—whatever catches my eye—when I am hiking. These I keep on my vanity.

Whatever you collect on your travels represents the layers of your life. Why not surround yourself with all your best memories?

**PREVIOUS PAGE:** Hans Wegner Elbow chairs, mid-century classics, keep things light and comfortable around the custom resin dining table, which channels the essential angles of this house into softer undulations. The light fixture from Studio Twenty Seven makes its own quiet statement overhead as it refers to the steel elements of the architecture. The photographs are by Bruno Augsburger.

**RIGHT:** The play of curves, angles, and interlinks comes to the fore in the media room on the other side of the fireplace structure. The sweeping arc of the custom, velvet-covered sofa combines with the ceiling paper by Porto Teleo, multilevel plushness of the rug from Azadi, Adam Birch's carved wood squiggle of a coffee table, the screen by Londubh Studio, and curtain fabric by Élitis to turn up the groovy quotient to full blast.

OPPOSITE: The commissioned screen from Londubh Studio takes design cues from the curtain fabric and adds a disco metallic twist to complexify the dance of light around the room. ABOVE, LEFT: A Joe Colombo lounge chair has a space-age air that feeds right into the media room's aesthetic beat. ABOVE, RIGHT: Adam Birch, a South African artist, shaped the coffee table from a solid piece of wood.

PREVIOUS PAGES: Degrees of matte and sheen play across the kitchen's patinated steel hood, soapstone island, tile wall, and leather stools. The pendant fixtures from Marset give off a gorgeous amber glow when lit. THIS PAGE: When I saw these ceramics in Turkey, I immediately pictured them against this backdrop. OPPOSITE: In all its variegated darkness, the kitchen serenely anchors one end of the visually active living space. FOLLOWING PAGES: The client asked that his bedroom be done in Weimaraner gray. PAGE 142: Artist Caroline Lizarraga created the mural. The chairs are by the Beirut-based studio David/Nicolas. PAGE 143: Custom wool and cashmere curtain panels infuse shades of amethyst for contrast. The sheers are a fashion fabric.

**ABOVE:** This guest bedroom is dubbed "Lenny's Room" for several reasons; chief among them is that the wallpaper is from Lenny Kravitz's design studio. The scale of the curtain pattern and the check of the bed throw balance the wallpaper's gigantic forms. **OPPOSITE:** The wallpaper from Voutsa gives the second guest bedroom a really happy vibe.

**PREVIOUS PAGES:** A vintage 1970s-era suede, chrome, and wood bar by Willy Rizzo, custom wall mural and églomisé mirror by Caroline Lizarraga, custom sectional, and newly reupholstered vintage club chairs transformed this space off the pool into the opium den of the client's dreams. **RIGHT:** Even the pool area has a groovy, space-age vibe. The opium den creates a seamless party space for indoor/outdoor entertaining, and also makes the most of the fabulous hillside setting.

# SHORT STORY

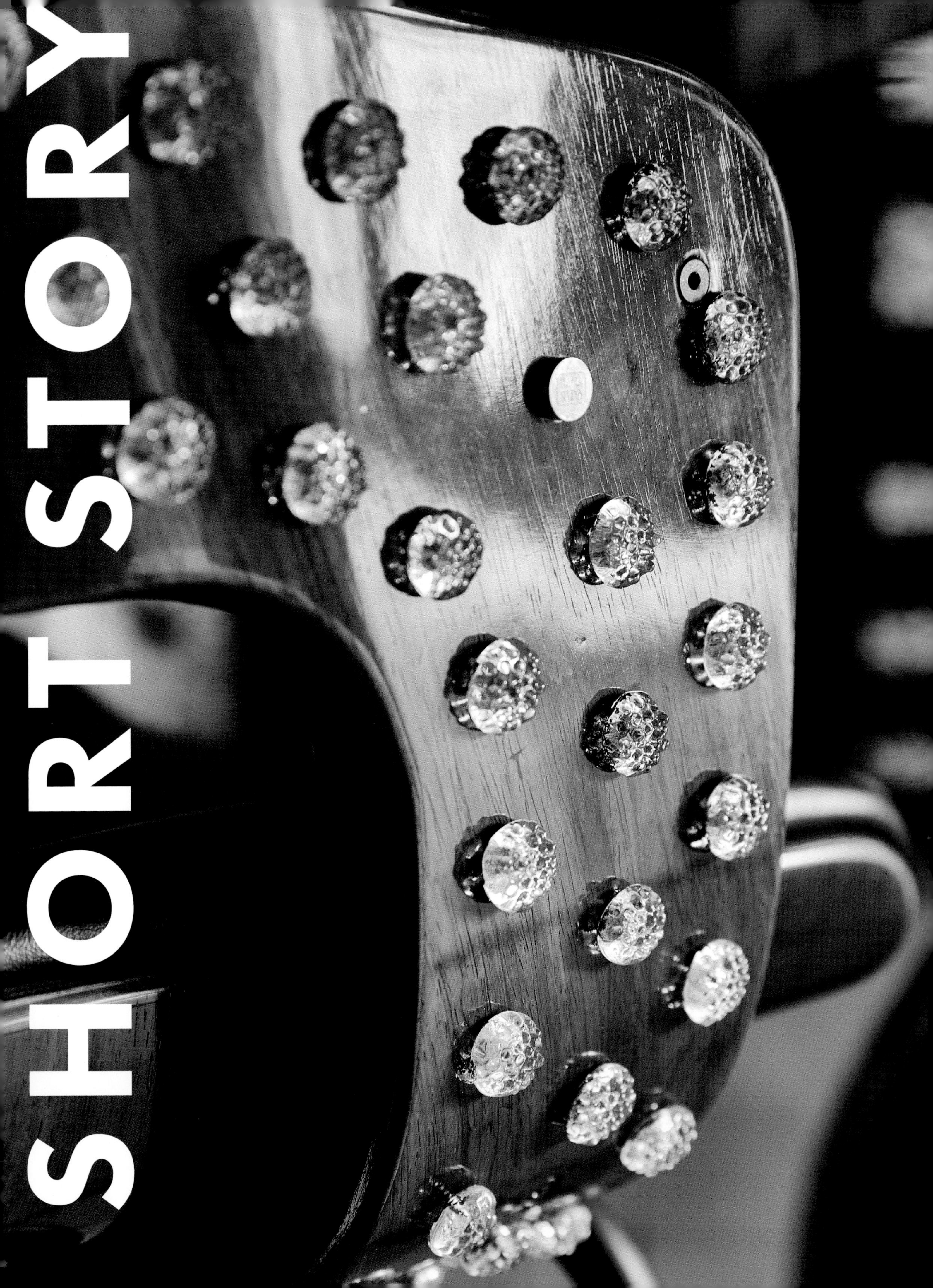

The best thing about **SHOW HOUSE** rooms is that you can be so **FUN, IMAGINA-TIVE, AND EXPERIMENTAL.** You dream up the client. You play with unusual combinations, try new design directions, and curate the space. Something about the light and proportions of this room in the *Galerie* House of Art & Design made it **AN INNATELY HAPPY SPACE.** I saw it as a study, a very sexy, cocoon-like lounge for a connoisseur of art and travel.

**WRAPPING AN ENTIRE ROOM IN PATTERNED WALLCOVERING** was a departure for me, but the effect of the Fromental design I chose, which looks like eggshells, **FELT COMPLETELY EMBRACING.** We extrapolated the pattern from the wallpaper for the fireplace mantel. I like the combination of red and black, so I lacquered the ceiling to match the wallcovering. The light floor and rug balance the intensity.

I am **ALWAYS ON THE HUNT FOR UNIQUE PIECES.** The Brazilian desk chair bedazzled with little glass rosettes? To me, it's the furniture equivalent of a couture gown. The desk by Vincenzo De Cotiis and the light sculpture by Jorge Pardo bring in **CONTRAST-ING MATERIALS, TEXTURES, AND SHAPES.** The well-placed display niches—we deliberately rounded the edges—carry on this **DIALOGUE OF GEOMETRIES.**

That this show house was all about art and design allowed me to **CURATE A COLLEC-TION** of pieces by Sanford Biggers, Marcel Dzama, Rashid Johnson, and others. Favorites from my own stash of barware and smoking items add the personal touch. These things are **MEANINGFUL TO ME—AND TO THE PERSON I IMAGINED LIVING THERE.**

**OPPOSITE:** The vintage Brazilian desk chair brings incredible artistry to the room. **FOLLOWING PAGES:** The Fromental wallpaper and painted ceiling create an all-embracing environment for artwork of various kinds. A George Condo work feels at home over the marble fireplace. Christophe Côme's fireplace screen expands the conversation about art and design.

**ABOVE, LEFT TO RIGHT:** The slatted backs of mid-century Brazilian lounge chairs by Martin Eisler echo a geometric motif that recurs throughout this space in different variations. A vintage bar cart is home to some pieces of barware from my own collections. This ceramic by William J. O'Brien feels like it was made just for this room. Totemic onyx sculptures by Cesare Arduini found at Maison Gerard bring glow and focus to one corner.

**IT'S A LUXURY TO LIVE IN A GORGEOUSLY DESIGNED HOME,** especially when it's historic, but it means you are obligated to pay attention to its original intention. This house has only had three owners since Winthrop Gilman Jr., who coincidentally lived on Gramercy Park, as we do, built it as a country getaway in 1874. When my husband and I first saw it, it was in serious disrepair. The front door was nailed shut. There were mushrooms growing in the entry hall. We couldn't walk up even one flight of stairs because they were covered in shards of glass. But after five minutes in the house, we knew.

**WITH AN OLD HOUSE, YOU HAVE TWO CHOICES.** You can **PRESERVE** everything possible and try to make anything new look like it was always there. **OR** you can **MAKE YOUR OWN MARK.** We didn't want to compete with the traditional elements, so anything new we put in, like the stair and the kitchens, we made very modern. We kept the basic layout the same because the house had great bones and the flow of the floor plan felt clear, organic, and gracious. The high ceilings with their original ornate plaster detail were so beautiful, and the rooms were perfectly proportioned, expansive enough for large gatherings, but easy to furnish for intimacy.

**THE SENSIBILITY** of these rooms was **INSPIRED BY COPENHAGEN,** where I had been spending a lot of time. I began with lighting, as I so often do, and here the fixtures tend to be more contemporary, and mostly from Sweden, Finland, and Italy. To conjure up what I had felt in the hotels and homes of Denmark, I went with wide plank floors and white plaster walls. And then I layered in coziness with felt, pelts, leather, and textiles. The furniture combines vintage pieces—I love the hunt—with pieces I had made to fit.

**THE DINING ROOM** is a very fun place to give dinner parties, and special to us because of the installation we commissioned from the Austrian artist Otto Zitko. **BECAUSE THE WALLS ARE SO LOUD, I WANTED EVERYTHING ELSE IN THE ROOM TO BE VERY QUIET.** The materials are all natural. The custom table is made from Belgian oak. The ceramics, which I found in a small town in Provence, feel right at home with the installation.

**THE KITCHENS** here are organized almost **LIKE THOSE IN ASIA,** where it is not uncommon to have a dry kitchen and a wet kitchen. The wet kitchen, where the hard work goes on, can serve as a catering kitchen; the dry kitchen is for every-day cooking and the finishing details for entertaining.

We wanted **A BIG BATHROOM WITH A FIREPLACE,** so we converted a bedroom and turned the side rooms into dressing rooms, connecting them with oak millwork. The glassed-in shower in the round? It's a showpiece, and I'm still not sure what prompted it. Maybe the fact that it was both a fascinating design challenge and a feat of technical precision made it **IRRESISTIBLE.**

In this house, there are objects from a family safari in Africa, textiles from a trip to Chile, match strikers and barware from all over Europe, and ceramics from all over Asia. As I get older, I feel that **HAVING TOO MANY THINGS CAN WEIGH YOU DOWN. BUT A CURATED COLLECTION EDITED TO HOLD YOUR MEMORIES CLOSE TELLS YOUR FAMILY STORY.**

**PAGE 157:** The dining room is one of our happy places. **OPPOSITE:** Cy Twombly's apartment in Rome inspired the entry floor. Artworks by Yayoi Kusama, left, and Jonas Wood, right, bring the quiet gallery to life. **FOLLOWING PAGES, LEFT:** We enhanced the exterior, replicated the original front doors, and reused the original knockers. **FOLLOWING PAGES, RIGHT:** Custom metal vestibule doors add to the interior's slow reveal.

OPPOSITE: The stair is one of the most visible meeting points of the historic house and our modern reinvention. ABOVE: A vintage Swedish settee gives us a cozy spot to contemplate the Kusama painting. FOLLOWING PAGES: Art by Sterling Ruby, left, and Jim Lambie, right, help fill this area of our neutral living room with warmth. The designs of Pierre Paulin inspired my custom sofas. The side chairs are twentieth-century Brazilian classics by Carlo Hauner and Martin Eisler.

**ABOVE:** One of Rashid Johnson's shea butter pieces adds interest and function. **OPPOSITE:** A detail of the stone and metal coffee table by Dutch sculptor Paul Kingma, a perfect home for one of Roger Herman's ceramics. **FOLLOWING PAGES:** I want art to capture my eye—and my imagination—wherever it travels in space, but without overwhelming. That's why I tend to keep the other elements of my rooms comparatively quiet.

# MOOD MATTERS

Our bodies react to our surroundings. This is why the atmosphere of each room—and the overall home—matters so very much. My goal is to create environments that are comfortable, enjoyable, and welcoming. I spend a great deal of time thinking through each element of a room, and the effect these elements create together. A room filled only with fabulous, famous items can be intimidating, with a look-but-don't-touch vibe. I love these kind of brand-name pieces with a big presence, too. And I use them with joy. But I work very hard to make them friendly, to bring them into a warm, relaxed, enveloping fold.

Contrast is key. I'm attracted to duality. When the very fragile meets the concrete, when the delicate pairs with the precision engineered, when the rough meets the sleek and the plush, and you add in a touch of the fancy and just the right art, you can create a chemistry that is more than just visual.

Lighting sets a tone, which I see as one of design's most important aspects. The right fixture can become just the right focal point. In this way, lighting, which is always utilitarian, also serves as a piece of art, a functional sculpture that performs an outsized role by setting a space's entire mood.

There are so many incredible lighting fixtures available, both contemporary and vintage, in every scale and style. Artists and craftspeople continue to push this age-old medium forward with unexpected forms and surprising materials—the natural, the man-made, the high, the low—everything from textiles, twigs, and paper cups to LED bulbs. Murano's master artisans still craft some of the most beautiful fixtures ever, using glass-blowing techniques from hundreds and hundreds of years ago.

For me, lighting is the life of the room, the energy of the space. We all have strong opinions about the sofa: that it needs to be comfortable and durable for children and pets. But unlike a sofa, no one actually touches the overhead lighting. It is one of design's great workhorses—and for me, often makes the entire room.

PAGE 171: An Ico Parisi fixture marks the dining room entry with whimsy. PREVIOUS PAGES, LEFT: A sculpture by Sarah Lucas encapsulates the room's contrasts in a single statement. PREVIOUS PAGES, RIGHT: So graphic in daylight, Otto Zitko's mural transforms at night. OPPOSITE: The custom Belgian oak table is the room's calm center. THIS PAGE: Calvin Klein candlesticks add pinpoints of sheen. Timothée Humbert's ceramic brings the outdoors inside.

PREVIOUS PAGES, LEFT: One of two kitchens, this L-shaped space works for family meals and dinner party staging. The light fixture is by Paavo Tynell. A Japanese felt vessel inserts rustic refinement amid the polish. PREVIOUS PAGES, RIGHT: Ample storage space here allows for easy table setting in the dining room. ABOVE: Kirk Hayes's painting challenges in pretty pastels. OPPOSITE: The Ginori tableware talks pattern and color with the de Gournay pitcher and bowl.

With a custom banquette and a vintage table, this cozy corner of the living room is where we hang out and play all sorts of board and card games. It's also the perfect spot for putting out snacks when we're entertaining. The photo by Richard Prince introduces a punk note into the peaceful setting.

**ABOVE, LEFT TO RIGHT:** In a nod to James Turrell, an inset sconce above the banquette has an LED bulb that changes color on rotation. **FOLLOWING PAGES:** Stripping the walls of their paneling was a key step in transforming this former library into our cheerful, light-filled family room. From left to right, the artworks are by Raymond Pettibon, Lisa Yuskavage, and Etel Adnan.

YAYOI KUSAMA

JAY OR

YAYOI KUSAMA

CALDER

HOWGATE

LUCIAN FREUD PORTRAITS

PACE

Yale

PREVIOUS PAGES, LEFT: The metal inlay
is a cool understated detail on
the side table; its stained wood grain
resonates against the pale oak floor
from Copenhagen. PREVIOUS PAGES,
RIGHT: The silk-and-wool rug adds a
touch of shimmer. OPPOSITE: French
tables puzzle together and pull apart
when necessary. THIS PAGE: Cody
Hoyt's ceramic and eggs of various
materials play with the geometric
details of the mantel.

I decided to hang Jeremy Demester's fantastic, large painting in my husband's office because it reminds me so much of him: he, just like the figure depicted, has a nonstop stream of beautiful ideas flowing out from his brain. The vintage leather chair is one of a pair, and just so comfortable.

**ABOVE:** Match strikers bring color to the coffee table. **OPPOSITE:** I prefer my upholstered pieces petite and low, so I designed this sectional to hug the corner at windowsill height. Made with old book jackets, Sam Falls's artwork captures my husband's passion for reading.
**FOLLOWING PAGES:** Our second-floor landing becomes a gallery space with art by Jonathan Meese, left, Brian Calvin, center, and Tal R, right.

In soft, pale blue-grays and other light neutral shades, our bedroom is a serene haven that feels nested amid the treetops. The furnishings have an understated mid-century vibe with a burled veneer bed by Paul Evans, overhead fixture by Max Ingrand, standing lamp by Isamu Noguchi, and lounge chairs by Osvaldo Borsani. The painting by Tal R feels just right for this space.

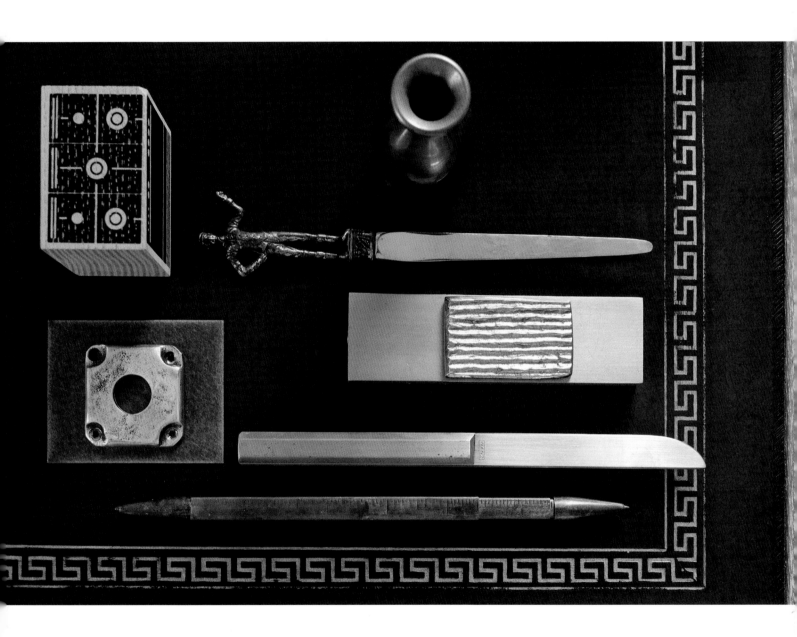

**OPPOSITE:** My office is a home to favorite pieces, including this chair-like sculpture by the Argentine artist Alexandra Kehayoglou. Custom-woven silk curtains diffuse light. **ABOVE:** My French antique desk hosts paper-related implements. **FOLLOWING PAGES, LEFT:** Ebonized wood and brass handles bring sculptural detail to the bar. The artwork is by Cecily Brown. **FOLLOWING PAGES, RIGHT:** A Japanese ceramic seems to bloom in the linen closet adjacent.

PREVIOUS PAGES: Our primary bath is an "if you dream it, we will build it" experiment in design and engineering. I love the contrast in the figuring of the Paonazzo marble that sheathes the wet areas of the room. THIS PAGE: The architectural ceiling fixture by Vincenzo De Cotiis casts such captivating light. OPPOSITE: The wood elements add nature's warmth into the mix.

There are some projects—this one included—that I think of as "only in New York" stories. **IMAGINE LIVING EYE LEVEL WITH OR ABOVE THE CLOUDS,** with 360-degree views of the skyscape, as this client does. Picture your everyday backdrop is the Empire State Building's spire and other iconic building tops, which is this client's experience. Obviously, I had to **FIND WAYS TO USE DESIGN TO BRING THE FOCUS BACK INSIDE.** This client's love of bright, saturated colors—Yves Klein blue, hot pink, and chrome yellow—helped us accomplish that. Expanses of cloud-bright white balance the hues, which shift throughout the interior.

An art collector with edgy taste, this client truly appreciates contemporary furniture design. For this reason, **EACH PIECE HAD TO HAVE ITS OWN STORY AND A STRONG POINT OF VIEW.** I made the individual selections with an eye to creating a very curated collection. The entry console designed by Mathieu Lehanneur, the French artist and designer, fits the bill, for example. It's functional and sculptural, and its glass base illuminates. With artwork by Julie Mehretu above and a Jeff Koons sculpture on top, it becomes even more special. Because the foyer is between the dining and living rooms, if the client is entertaining, this art piece can also become a buffet table.

In the living room, touches of hot pink and blue splash into the whiteness. I designed a sweeping curved sofa to take advantage of the stunning views and positioned the vintage lounge chairs by Osvaldo Borsani to do the same. Paul Cocksedge, an art student whose work I saw at a gallery in Chelsea, created the living room light fixture, which looks like it's made of Dixie cups but is folded pieces of paper. This fixture resonates with the nearby wall sculpture by the Korean artist Chun Kwang Young, which is almost like papier-mâché.

PAGE 209: The Julie Mehretu painting, Jeff Koons sculpture, and Mathieu Lehanneur console each tell a story. Together in the entry, they speak powerfully about what's to come. PREVIOUS PAGES: The client's love of bold color helps draw focus back to the interior. Thank you, Yves Klein, for your brilliant blue—and for the iconic coffee table that centers this seating area. THESE PAGES: The contours of the custom sofa embrace the view. The photograph of glaciers is by Frank Thiel.

**THE IDEA OF PIXELATION IS ANOTHER UNIFYING THEME.** A pair of Chuck Close paintings in the front hallway and dining room speak to a kind of twentieth-century pointillism. Behind the dining room table hangs an artwork by Zhuang Hong Yi with a surface covered in small ceramic petals that, when viewed from different angles, change from magenta to blue.

To make sure each client gets exactly the dining table they want, I'll often design a table just for them and have it made, as I did here. It was impossible to find a single slab long enough for the space, so I created metal brackets to join the marble sections that correlate with the metal details on the chair backs. The table was so large and sculptural, we had to assemble all the pieces on site.

The kitchen, with just a few revisions, became the interior's palette cleanser. Here we changed the marble to white and introduced the pops of yellow that extend deep into the TV room in the seating and millwork.

The primary bedroom, though serene in spirit, captivates with art and whimsy. We reached out to Jimmie Martin, a graffiti artist whose work the client had seen and loved in London, to transform a Queen Anne–style burr desk into an avant-garde vanity with a spray-painted surface. We even brought the art motif into the boys' bedrooms with Cy Twombly–inspired wallpaper. **HIGH IN THE SKY, THE SPACES ARE FUN, BRIGHT, AND BOLD.**

**OPPOSITE:** A pumpkin modeled after Yayoi Kusama's artwork inserts a yellow splash. **FOLLOWING PAGES:** Artworks by Zhuang Hong Yi, left, and Chuck Close, right, shock the dining room with dynamic color and texture. We constructed the custom table on site; its metal joints relate to the chair details. **PAGES 218–219:** The ceramic petals on the surface of Zhuang Hong Yi's artwork change color depending on the viewer's position.

**OPPOSITE:** Another of Chuck Close's self-portraits commands one vista from the entry hall. As arresting as the painting is on its own terms, it is also intrinsic to the interior's color story: the jacket inspired the use of yellow. **ABOVE:** Linen curtains help cocoon the TV room when desired.

**ABOVE:** Bert Stern's photograph adds an edge into the ethereal primary bedroom. **OPPOSITE, LEFT:** Graffiti artist Jimmie Martin transformed the wife's vanity. **OPPOSITE, RIGHT:** The primary bath is a cloud of whiteness. **FOLLOWING PAGES, LEFT:** Cy Twombly–inspired wallpaper and a Jean-Michel Basquiat reproduced on skateboards bring the art into the boys' bedrooms.
**FOLLOWING PAGES, RIGHT:** In one, cushioned fabric wall paneling, a custom bed, and a cushy chair create a cozy nest.

**EVERY HOUSE IS ITS OWN STORY.** Many factors—including the client's taste, lifestyle, and history; the setting; the architecture—help shape the narrative. Working on new construction, like this courtyard house that architects Lake|Flato nested into the Colorado foothills, gives you an amazing opportunity to mold each last detail. I was involved from the beginning, so I was able to weigh in on all the interior finishes, which give the rooms so much of their character. All of us agreed that **INSIDE AND OUT, THIS HOUSE** should be **AT ONE WITH THE LANDSCAPE,** so we **FOCUSED ON** its **MATERIALITY.**

To create the **EARTHY, TEXTURAL, ORGANIC INTERIOR SPACES** we imagined, we selected stone floors, limestone, board-form concrete, and wood. But because these finishes together can be **A BIT AUSTERE,** I decided to **CREATE WARMTH WITH TEXTURE** and with **ART,** which I curated from around the world. I also designed much of the furniture. And as I almost always do, I included a percentage of vintage pieces, like the living room's woven leather Danish chairs, for depth and patina.

**THE MIX EVOLVES FROM ROOM TO ROOM, FROM PLACE TO PLACE.** One of the first pieces I chose was for the living room: Jean-Pierre Viot's ceramic coffee table. It's both organic and sleek, and its inlays helped dictate some of the selections of art. I love those **POPS OF COLOR,** which come straight from nature. Plus, the sheen of the glaze added a nice bit of reflection. The ceramic side table by Maarten Stuer, in contrast, is so rough, matte, and sculptural, it becomes almost like a work of brutalist architecture in miniature. The mohair-covered sofas,

**PAGE 226:** The entry gallery introduces the palette of forms, textures, and materials that give this house its character. **PAGES 228–229:** Lake|Flato's design feels organic to the landscape. **PREVIOUS PAGES:** Seamless transitions between the interior and exterior keep nature always spectacularly in the frame. **RIGHT:** With views in both directions, the living room is inviting yet quiet. Together, the furnishings embody the interior's every motif: rough, smooth, brutalist, finessed, polished, matte, luxe—the whole shebang. Mohair-covered custom sofas create an inviting conversation area in front of the fireplace. A plush rug ups the lushness amid the harder surfaces. An artwork by Jordy Kerwick above the mantel picks up the pastels in the top of the coffee table. Vintage walnut lamps flank the fireplace.

**ABOVE:** Maarten Stuer's ceramic side tables, which remind me of brutalist architecture in miniature, echo the texture and feel of the board-form concrete elements elsewhere in the house. **OPPOSITE:** Jean-Pierre Viot's ceramic coffee table makes such an interesting comment on the push-pull of man-made vs. nature-made that reoccurs throughout this interior. The colors of the insets influenced our choice of artwork.

which we made, along with the vintage lamps and chairs, brought in **LUSHNESS AND HISTORY.** In the library, we shifted the balance with subdued colors and **HEIGHTENED FORMS, SHAPES, AND TEXTURES, ALL OF WHICH RELATE TO THE LANDSCAPE** in one way or another. The media room became a luxurious cocoon with wall panels wrapped in a Japanese textile and inviting textures, including mohair, woven leather, and stone. For the primary suite, we kept things **PEACEFUL AND SERENE.**

With **NATURE ALWAYS ON VIEW,** I looked for **WORKS OF ART THAT MET ITS MAJESTY—AND THE CHARACTER OF EACH SPACE.** I knew a large ceramic by Kazunori Hamana would be just right in the entry but decided to elevate it on a lacquer pedestal so that it would get the proper attention. On the opposing wall I pictured a sculptural element, which I found from the Texas artist Otis Jones. A hand-carved bench by Adam Birch added a personal note: it was made in South Africa, where the client once lived. To command the white plaster wall off the entry, a large, graphic, abstract work by Serge Alain Nitegeka made sense from the start. For the dining room, I found a painting by Tomory Dodge loaded with color, so pretty, cheerful, and happy. The tapestry in the hall to the master suite, which came from Beirut, added in another layer of texture. I used ceramics from many different makers to provide the grace notes.

## NATURAL, ORGANIC, PEACEFUL: THIS IS THEIR LANDSCAPE OF HOME.

**OPPOSITE:** With its mix of beehive-like ceramic diffusers, the light fixture from BDDW that hovers over the marble library table brings the outside inside in such an understated way. **FOLLOWING PAGES:** Like most of the furnishings, the pull-up chairs, leather-covered banquette, and table are my designs.

**OPPOSITE:** As we refined the plans, we dedicated certain wall spaces and framed specific interior views to create dramatic art reveals. With its arresting abstract work by Serge Alain Nitegeka, this expanse opposite the entry is key to the unfolding experience of the interior. **ABOVE:** The powder room is a study in restraint. The sconce's wood slats filter the light so beautifully.

**ABOVE:** The wood tabletop radiates warmth. **OPPOSITE:** Sculptural lacquer armchairs expand on the table's lacquer detail. Vintage wood side chairs add contrast with comfort. The colors in Tomory Dodge's painting could have been pulled from outside. **FOLLOWING PAGES:** With its palette of pale greens and warm whites, the primary bedroom practically merges into the landscape. Alex Prager's photo creates a strong focal point.

**OPPOSITE:** The custom carved walnut headboard wraps the bed in a warm, solid embrace. **ABOVE:** A large tapestry brings its texture, warmth, and graphic pulse to the bedroom hallway. **FOLLOWING PAGES:** The media room luxuriates in textures that range in plushness from the Japanese textile that wraps the wall panels to the rug's deep pile, from the mohair-dressed sofa to the woven leather and marble side tables.

**OPPOSITE:** A graphic bedspread and leather-and-wood chairs radiate warmth in the guest bedroom. **ABOVE:** The pillow pattern ties together the grid of the honed stone wall, the contrasting channeling of the headboard, and the palette of the bedspread. **FOLLOWING PAGES:** The pool area nestles neatly into the flatlands that abut the framing hillsides.

# ACKNOWLEDGMENTS

This book is for:

KEN GARSCHINA, my HUSBAND, my biggest FAN, and BELIEVER in my talent, who always PUSHES ME TO BE MY BEST.

MARY JEAN SHAH, my MOTHER, who TAUGHT me the BEAUTY IN NATURE and ART.

ED STORY, my FATHER, who GAVE ME my LAUGHTER and LOVE OF LIFE.

JOSEPHINE STORY, who TAUGHT OUR FAMILY HOW TO SAY, "I LOVE YOU."

GAUTAM SHAH, who has GIVEN OUR FAMILY so much LOVE and ADVENTURE.

My SISTERS, LISA STORY and KATIE WOLD; their HUSBANDS, PHIL KAPLAN AND CHAD WOLD; and their CHILDREN, EMILY KAPLAN, ETHAN KAPLAN, and STORY KIMURA.

BRIAN GARRETT and STEPHEN FRONK, my BEST FRIENDS and PARTNERS IN ADVENTURE AND FUN, who are always FILLED WITH LAUGHTER and LOVE.

My OGS, the FRIENDS who are FAMILY: NANCY RIVIERE, KRISSY JOHNSTON, TRACY REINES, TODD JOYCE, HALLEH AMIRI, JESSICA HAWKINS, and EDWARD RODWELL.

KATE DOERGE, KAREN DUFFY, and NICOLE GREENE, MY FIRST MOM FRIENDS, who became MY BEST FRIENDS.

STACEY GOERGEN, my MENTOR in the NEW YORK ART WORLD and DEAR FRIEND.

FAWN GALLI, my DESIGN PARTNER IN CRIME who spreads MAGIC wherever she goes.

To MIKE MEDRANO, THANK YOU for making my MORNING WORKOUTS the BEST PART of MY DAY.

To CHRISTOPHER-JOHN and JORDAN SPARKES, MY GLAM SQUAD, who make EVERY DAY A FABULOUS HAIR DAY.

To my GRAMERCY CREW: CARMELA DOLFI, ZITA LAFUENTE, EDNA SACAYLE, and CHRISTIAN REYES for making my HOME LIFE FULL OF LOVE.

THIS BOOK would not have been possible without the AMAZING JILL COHEN and the INCREDIBLE TEAM: MELISSA POWELL, JUDITH NASATIR, DOUG TURSHEN, and STEVE TURNER. As well as THE FANTASTIC WORK OF PHOTOGRAPHERS JOSHUA MCHUGH and ROGER DAVIES. THANK YOU everyone at RIZZOLI for BELIEVING IN ME, especially CHARLES MIERS, PUBLISHER, and my EDITOR, KATHLEEN JAYES.

ALL OF THESE PROJECTS came to FRUITION with the TALENTED TEAM AT SSD. MY RIGHT HAND, PAULA HEAP FOLEY, and my WONDERFUL DESIGN CREW: KRISTINE BURGESS, ARIELLE O'CONNOR, and my SSD OG, ANDREA TSANGARIS.

I AM GRATEFUL to all the MAGAZINES and the fantastic EDITORS who have supported my work: AMY ASTLEY and ALISON LEVASSEUR at ARCHITECTURAL DIGEST; LISA COHEN and JACQUELINE TERREBONNE AT GALERIE; INGRID ABRAMOVITCH at ELLE DECOR; PAMELA JACCARINO at LUXE INTERIORS + DESIGN; STEELE MARCOUX at VERANDA; and CINDY ALLEN at INTERIOR DESIGN.

FOR ALL MY DEAR CLIENTS, PAST, PRESENT, and FUTURE: THANK YOU FOR TRUSTING ME WITH YOUR DREAMS, WHICH LET ME LIVE MINE.